A Pi. BOOK BY DEBRA ADAMS

STARS OF
BEVERLY HILLS,
90210

Debra Adams is a freelance writer whose entertainment and sports stories have appeared nationally.

CONTENTS

THE MAKING OF BEVERLY HILLS 90210

Cast member Tori Spelling poses with her famous father, producer Aaron Spelling, whose company is partially responsible for the production of *Beverly Hills, 90210*.

Finally.

From the multitude of television series geared toward today's high-school teenagers, one program has at last hit the airwaves that gets an A+ from teens around the world. It's cool, it's sassy, it's funny, it's honest, but most of all, it's believable. *Beverly Hills, 90210* has become the hippest and hottest teen-oriented show on the tube today.

With the help of ace producer Aaron Spelling—legendary for such TV ratings busters as *Charlie's Angels, Dynasty, The Love Boat,* and *Fantasy Island*—*Beverly Hills, 90210* has beaten the odds by appealing not only to teenagers but also to younger kids, young adults, and single women. In other words, it appeals to audiences of all ages, and the show's ratings reflect this. But, it is the teen audience who has taken the show to heart.

In the last couple of seasons, several teen-oriented series made their debuts, including *Tribes, Parker Lewis Can't Lose, Hull High,* and *Ferris Bueller.* Each tried to capture the teen market by focusing on the trials and tribulations of high-school life. Unfortunately, most missed the mark by a mile: They depended too much on silly characters; they were too unbelievable; or, they were too dull. *Beverly Hills, 90210* isn't like those other shows because it has what they obviously lacked—class, honesty, and a talented cast!

What is it about *Beverly Hills, 90210* that makes millions of people around the world (the show is broadcast in ten countries, and is number one in England!) tune in each week? How has this teen phenomenon become a real ratings grabber, snatching thousands of viewers away from its top-rated rival, *Cheers?* The answer involves a combination of the show's cast, its sympathetic treatment of teenagers, and its believable storylines. The show's success, the creators explain, is due to its appealing honesty. "No one," creator/coproducer Darren Star told *TV Guide,* "had done a truthful, sophisticated show about high school that would speak to kids the way *thirtysomething* spoke to its generation." From the show's drop-dead gorgeous cast to its hip, timely plots, *Beverly Hills, 90210* has the winning combination—and the winning ratings.

When the idea for *Beverly Hills, 90210* was first presented, the series was titled *Class of Beverly Hills.* The show's creator, Darren Star, and executive producer, Charles Rosin, anticipated a humble beginning and were happy to get respectable but modest ratings. Much to their surprise, what they got was a sleeper hit with some awesome ratings! To distinguish the series from other teen-oriented programs, the production team wanted to give it a recognizable identity—a memorable hook. So early

In the same season that *Beverly Hills, 90210* debuted, several other teen-related series also debuted, including *Parker Lewis Can't Lose.*

Among the shows that also competed for the attention of teenagers was NBC's *Hull High,* starring Cheryl Pollack and Mark Ballou, among others. The series' odd mix of teen drama with musical numbers was obviously inspired by MTV, but few viewers appreciated the experiment, and *Hull High* disappeared from NBC's lineup.

5

James at 15, starring Lance Kerwin, was one of the first series to take teenagers and their problems seriously. It premiered in 1977.

Room 222 (1969-74), like *Beverly Hills, 90210*, used a high-school setting as a focus for exploring important social issues.

on, the show's title was changed to include the zip code of America's most exclusive community. The gimmick worked, and now the show is commonly referred to as *90210* by regular viewers.

Beverly Hills, 90210 focuses on the lives of fraternal twins Brenda and Brandon Walsh (Shannen Doherty and Jason Priestley), who were transplanted from their middle-class Minneapolis hometown to the rich and famous rolling hills of Beverly. The Walshes moved not by choice, but by necessity. When Jim Walsh (James Eckhouse) was transferred from the Minneapolis branch of his international accounting firm to its Beverly

Hills office, he packed up his family and reluctantly moved west. Out of their element in snobby Beverly Hills, the family struggles to adjust to a new and sometimes alien lifestyle. While parents Jim and Cindy Walsh (Carol Potter) tend to fight their surroundings, teenagers Brandon and Brenda try to fit in.

As registered students of the wealthy and snooty West Beverly Hills High, Brandon and Brenda have found fitting in is not always easy. Despite the parking lot full of Porsches and the dress code of designer clothes, West Beverly Hills High has some of the same problems and obstacles that plague any suburban high school. The students run the gamut from jocks to burn-outs, from snobs to scholars, and Brandon and Brenda have had to find their niche in West Beverly High's social order.

Keeping Brandon and Brenda company are a diverse gang of Beverly Hills teens. Friends include handsome Dylan McKay (Luke Perry), the soft-spoken son of extremely wealthy but distant parents; sophisticated Kelly Taylor (Jennie Garth), who harbors dark secrets about her home life; spoiled Steve Sanders (Ian Ziering), another member of the elite set who is more impressed with hot wheels and hot babes than anything else; brainy Andrea Zuckerman (Gabrielle Carteris), the sweet-natured editor of the school newspaper; trendy Donna Martin (Tori Spelling), the style-conscious teen whose looks rank higher than her IQ; and pesty David "DJ" Silver (Brian Austin Green), the fun-loving freshman who would do anything to be one of the "in" crowd.

Life cruises in the fast lane for people who live in Beverly Hills, and Brenda and Brandon have witnessed or experienced many problems facing teens today—from alcoholism to suicide, from illness to divorce. By sticking close to their midwestern values, Brandon and Brenda have managed to handle any potentially sticky situation. The series' willingness to delve into serious teen-related issues has become a hallmark of

Jason Priestley stars as Brandon Walsh, a teenager whose family has moved from the Midwest to the posh community of Beverly Hills.

the show. In past episodes, Brenda discovered a lump in her breast, prompting some serious discussion on breast cancer; Kelly's mother admitted her problems with drugs and alcohol; Brandon discovered the folly of drinking and driving.

In this respect, *Beverly Hills, 90210*—like Fox Television's other teen drama, *21 Jump Street*—follows in the footsteps of some highly respected teen-related series of the past. *James at 15*, a critically acclaimed NBC series from the 1977-

A few sitcoms, including *Family Ties*, have attempted to address serious problems facing teens today. Here, Michael J. Fox, as Alex Keaton, talks things over with his girlfriend and his mom, played by Meredith Baxter Birney.

Most sitcoms, however, use teenagers and their problems just to get laughs. Though many loved *Happy Days*, the series was not often sympathetic or realistic in its portrayal of teens. From left: Ron Howard, Tom Bosley, and Henry Winkler.

1978 season, could be the direct forerunner of *90210*. The story of James Hunter, a teenager who is forced to move from rural Oregon to Boston when his father changes jobs, *James at 15* dealt with the problems James had with fitting into an urban high school. Certain episodes addressed day-to-day issues that all teens could relate to. For example, James turned 16 during the course of the first season, prompting a title change to *James at 16*, but the young man was frustrated because adults continued to treat him as a child. Other episodes explored more serious subjects, including James's first sexual experience.

Set primarily against a high-school backdrop, *Room 222* became a landmark TV series for its honest depiction of the problems facing America's youth during the late 1960s and early 1970s, an era

when the generation gap tore the country apart. In addition, many of the main characters were African-Americans, marking one of the few times that network television used black actors in important and three-dimensional roles. Though the comedy-drama focused more on social issues (including the antiwar sentiment, race relations, youth rebellion) than personal problems, teenagers closely related to the storylines.

Even such highly rated sitcoms as *Family Ties* and *The Cosby Show* have occasionally turned serious to focus on subjects relevant to teen audiences, including peer pressure, loyalty to friends and family, sex and romance, and taking responsibility for one's actions.

Another important feature that *Beverly Hills, 90210* has in common with all of these shows is a realistic, sympa-

An early success at Fox Television was *21 Jump Street*, which delved into such teen-related issues as drugs, gangs, and child abuse. From left: Dustin Nguyen, Holly Robinson, Peter DeLuise, Johnny Depp, and Steven Williams.

thetic portrayal of teenagers and their lives. Many TV programs, particularly such past sitcoms as *Happy Days* and *Welcome Back, Kotter*, presented ridiculous stereotypes of teenagers, usually from an adult's point of view. As one teen fan put it, "[*Beverly Hills, 90210* is] about things that really happen, not the stupid things they usually have on TV shows about teenagers."

Beverly Hills, 90210 has just begun its second season. Fox was so pleased with the response to the first season that the network ordered 30 more episodes, which should make their way into your living rooms well into 1992! Future episodes promise to be as thought-provoking as last season's. There is no question that future *Beverly Hills, 90210* storylines will have no boundaries, and die-hard fans can expect anything to happen!

One of the most popular storylines on *Beverly Hills, 90210* involves the hot romance between Dylan McKay (Luke Perry) and Brenda Walsh (Shannen Doherty). Viewers stayed glued to the set last season as the young couple explored the passion and heartbreak of a high-school romance. This plotline promises to heat up as Dylan goes through a family crisis and Brenda realizes she is deeply in love.

CAST OF CHARACTERS

BRANDON WALSH: JASON PRIESTLEY

BRENDA WALSH: SHANNEN DOHERTY

DYLAN McKAY: LUKE PERRY

STEVE SANDERS: IAN ZIERING

KELLY TAYLOR: JENNIE GARTH

DAVID "DJ" SILVER: BRIAN AUSTIN GREEN

ANDREA ZUCKERMAN: GABRIELLE CARTERIS

DONNA MARTIN: TORI SPELLING

BRANDON WALSH

Top and opposite: Soulful Brandon Walsh still holds to his midwestern values, which make him cautious about the glamorous, fast-paced lifestyle of Beverly Hills. In addition to going to school, Brandon works, which makes him different from other guys at West Beverly Hills High. He also shuns the designer threads of his fellow classmates in favor of more typical teen attire.

It sounds like a dream come true—leaving behind an average, ordinary life in the Midwest and moving to an exciting, new life in Beverly Hills, California. Despite what many of us may think, making the change from a middle-class neighborhood in Minnesota to an upper-crust community in California isn't as easy as it sounds. Thrust into the fast-paced world of the rich and famous, Brandon Walsh encounters one obstacle after another in his struggle to fit in.

Adjusting has been the most difficult part of the transition for Brandon. At first, this intelligent, good-natured teenager was overly eager to be accepted, resulting in his participation in some really stupid stunts, including drinking and driving. And, when he quit his summer job at the diner to work as a cabana boy at the swank Beverly Hills Beach Club, he didn't bother to give his former boss two weeks notice. The "old" Brandon from Minnesota would never have acted so irresponsibly. Luckily, when pangs of conscience began to bother him, the real Brandon emerged. He did the right thing by returning to the diner and offering to stay another week.

Green-eyed Brandon is not only brutally handsome, he is also sensitive. And, as far as brothers go, he is the ultimate! His love and understanding for his twin sister, Brenda, is obvious to everyone. He was there for her when she thought

she had a lump in her breast, giving her tremendous love and support. Ever so loyal, he remained by her side when she broke up with Dylan McKay—his closest friend. In Brandon's life, family comes first.

Not surprisingly, Brandon definitely has good luck with the girls, and the female residents of Beverly Hills have been more than kind to this innocent, corn-fed boy from the Midwest. Brandon occasionally provides some real shockers in terms of the dating scene, including the time he shared an intimate moment with the school newspaper editor and class brain, Andrea Zuckerman. When the two teens exchanged a blissfully romantic kiss, everyone rooted for this

unlikely high-school couple to get together. Unfortunately, the relationship never went any further, leaving all of us wondering literally what the story was.

Brandon also toyed with the notion of asking out trendy Kelly Taylor, though nothing ever came of this idea. With Brandon Walsh, there's no telling just which Beverly Hills beauty will finally win his heart!

This year, a more well-adjusted Brandon will go through additional changes—some good, some bad. Admittedly, this terrific teen does have a wild side, which may surface as the season moves along. As for girls in Brandon's life...a long-term relationship with anyone remains to be seen!

BRENDA WALSH

Top: Pretty Brenda Walsh is down to earth but has still managed to fit in at West Beverly Hills High.
Opposite left: Brenda and her twin brother, Brandon, protect and support each other in times of need.
Opposite right: Brenda attended the spring dance with her boyfriend Dylan McKay, a serious-minded but slightly rebellious student who is one of the hottest guys at West Beverly.

What a luxury to be young and beautiful in Beverly Hills. Unfortunately, girls in L.A.'s richest community are often not beautiful on the inside. It's a good thing that Brenda Walsh has her head on straight in the midst of all the glitz, glamour, and gauche.

Less than a year after moving to California from Minnesota, Brenda has found herself with a cool clique of friends, and with an even cooler boyfriend—sexy Dylan McKay. Life in Beverly Hills has had its ups and downs for the sassy 17-year-old, but, for the most part, she remains happy.

Despite her generally optimistic attitude, Brenda has witnessed the cruel side of life in the fast lane. More than once, her values have been put to the test, and, more than once, she has remained true to them. For example, at one point Brenda found herself envious of Kelly Taylor because of Kelly's beautiful, outgoing mother. She was frustrated that her own practical, down-to-earth mother wasn't as cool. Mrs. Taylor dressed to kill, stayed out all night at glamorous parties, and sat by the pool during the day—a real Beverly Hills mom. Brenda couldn't understand why her mom didn't want to live such a dazzling lifestyle.

But, an unpleasant turn of events snapped Brenda out of her jealousy and made her realize how wrong she had been. Mrs. Taylor was really an alcoholic and drug addict—a secret that Kelly had been hiding for years. "You don't know just how good you have it," she told Brenda. In finding out the truth about Kelly's mother, Brenda gained respect and admiration for her own mom.

On a more personal level, Brenda went through several sticky situations during the school year, including two very traumatic events. At one point, she thought

she might be pregnant; another time, she feared she might have breast cancer. Brenda faced both situations bravely, and all worked out in the end.

Dating the hottest guy at West Beverly Hills High has been a rollercoaster ride of emotions for Brenda. She loves the rebellious Dylan deeply—so much so that when she decided she needed time away from the relationship, she found breaking up with Dylan the hardest thing she'd ever done in her whole life. Strong-willed but stubborn, Brenda

resisted temptation in order to put her feelings in proper perspective. Finally, she realized she couldn't be without him.

Aside from Dylan, this long-haired beauty is not lacking for good friends. Like her charming twin brother, Brenda eventually adapted to her new surroundings, making several close pals in the process. Most often, she hangs with best friends Kelly Taylor and Donna Martin, though recently, she has befriended Andrea Zuckerman. Her friends mean the world to her, and Brenda never misses an opportunity to be there for any one of them.

DYLAN McKAY

Dylan McKay is not only drop-dead handsome but also serious and intelligent. He can also be trouble, particularly for adults. Dylan is the classic case of the teenager who is rebellious on the outside and troubled on the inside.

The soft-spoken, dreamy intellect of the West Beverly posse, Dylan McKay would rather listen to classical music than go cruising with the boys. He's shy, but don't mistake that shyness for aloofness. Though many people see him as a rebel—even a troublemaker—those who know him know better.

Dylan is the son of mega-wealthy parents who divorced when he was six. He hails from the posh, opulent area of Beverly Hills, and he lives in a mansion so big that it embarrasses him. From looking at Dylan McKay, however, you would never guess that one day he stands to inherit a fortune. That's the way this handsome young dreamer is—money doesn't mean much to him.

In a recent and rather ironic turn of events, the McKays temporarily lost the wealth and status that made them so elite after his father was indicted for insider trading. Refusing to move to Hawaii to live with his mother, whom he hasn't seen in three years, Dylan is now on his own—with only his 1963 Porsche to his name.

Completely unspoiled, Dylan is the kind of guy who is not afraid to cry. He's sensitive, and he's not reluctant to show it. When girlfriend Brenda Walsh broke up with him because she wanted time apart from the relationship, a choked-up Dylan just couldn't hold back. "But, I love you," he sobbed, as his voice cracked and his eyes filled with tears. Who could resist such sincerity?

Recently, a glimpse of the real Dylan McKay emerged—not the angry, rebellious punk but a troubled soul who longs for the love and warmth of his parents. In a serious surfing accident, which occurred on the day of his father's arrest, Dylan cracked his ribs pretty badly. With his father in jail and his mother in Hawaii, there was no one to take care of him. Mrs. Walsh insisted that he stay with them and recuperate, though he was still reeling from his break-up with Brenda. With nowhere else to go, he made himself at home at the Walshes', sharing Brandon's room.

Dylan found it difficult to live under the same roof as his ex-girlfriend. In addition, he felt uncomfortable knowing that Mr. Walsh had never trusted him. But, during that time, he came to terms with much of the unpleasantness of his life. He managed to patch things up with both Brenda and Mr. Walsh, and he discovered his true feelings for his own father. In an emotionally moving moment, Dylan poured out his heart in a letter to his dad, professing hope that the two can be close again someday.

Best of all, near the end of Dylan's stay at the Walshes' house, love triumphed and the hottest couple at West Beverly Hills High got back together again!

Bitter over his parents' divorce and his father's lack of interest in him, the soft-spoken and sensitive Dylan shuns his family's wealthy status.

STEVE SANDERS

Spoiled, rich Steve Sanders is not as smart and sophisticated as he thinks he is. He fancies himself a real ladies man, but he can't seem to attract the lady that he wants—beautiful Kelly Taylor. Steve is more interested in hot cars and hot women than in serious relationships or meaningful values. No wonder Kelly lost interest in him.

Steve Sanders represents the perfect stereotype of the typical Beverly Hills dude. Born and raised in the swank Los Angeles community, where a person's popularity is dependent on his bank account, Steve professes that his main interests are hot women, hot cars, and hot clothes. It's life in the fast lane all the time for this handsome, curly-haired athlete.

But don't think for a minute that Steve has the ladies falling at his feet. In fact, Mr. Macho has not only had his share of flirtations but also his share of heartbreaks! In the past, he and fly girl Kelly Taylor were a hot and heavy item, and it's no secret that he still carries a torch for her. Too bad she won't give him the time of day!

Steve also made his move on Andrea Zuckerman, only to be instantly rejected. Dateless for the end-of-the-year spring dance, he ended up taking Donna Martin at the last minute.

If the truth be known, Steve just can't seem to get it together when it comes to the ladies. All that matters to this materialistic teen are looks and money. To make matters worse, Steve is a bad judge of character! Once, he and Brandon got taken in by two very attractive hustlers, who pulled a fast one on the boys. The sweet, innocent-looking girls were acting extremely friendly toward the guys when the pair climbed into

Steve's convertible to go for a ride. After the foursome got far enough away, one of the girls begged Steve for a lesson on how to drive a five-speed. When Brandon and Steve let the girls take the car for a spin by themselves, they never returned. Sometimes there are just too many potholes in the fast lane!

Steve's behavior is a reflection of his home life. The handsome young lad seems to be suffering from an identity crisis. This is one teen who would be lost in the real world, or anywhere outside his plastic environment. Mrs. Sanders, a celebrity with her own television show in which she plays a "perfect Mom" type, is anything but a perfect mother. In real life, she never finds time for her son.

In the meantime, Steve claims to be havin' a kickin' cool time just being a Beverly Hills hotshot! Part of the "in" crowd at school, Steve spends most of his spare time cruisin'. During the summer, with school closed and beaches open, Steve hit the surf and the volleyball court at the Beverly Hills Beach Club every single day. Occasionally, Steve does think of people other than himself, such as the time he helped good pal Brandon get a job as a cabana boy at the club. Still, he couldn't help wondering why anyone in their right mind would work during summer vacation!

Steve does pursue some sports, including tennis and volleyball at the Beverly Hills Beach Club. There he can keep an eye on Kelly, who can frequently be seen sunbathing at this exclusive club.

KELLY TAYLOR

Top: Kelly Taylor is the leader of West Beverly Hills High's most exclusive clique—a group she likes to call the "Brat Pack." Kelly's favorite activities include shopping for the kind of designer clothes that most girls only dream about and dishing the dirt on her fellow classmates. **Opposite:** Kelly tries to get rid of bothersome David "DJ" Silver, who is always trying to horn his way into the "Brat Pack."

Everyone at West Beverly Hills High School thinks Kelly Taylor has the perfect life with her smashing mod mansion, an incredibly trendy wardrobe, a prime cabana at the prestigious Beverly Hills Beach Club, and a totally cool relationship with her hip mom. But they don't know the real story.

For most of her high-school years, Kelly has been covering up a painful, dark secret. She has been struggling to hide the fact that her mother is an alcoholic and a drug addict. Unfortunately, this information became common knowledge last year on the night of the school fashion show. Mrs. Taylor, being the social butterfly that she is, had agreed to emcee. When she arrived at the fashion show, she was under the effects of cocaine, and she stumbled through her duties as emcee. Kelly watched in horror as her mother made a total fool of herself, obviously high on something. Unable to bear the cruel whispers and murmurs from the crowd, Kelly fled from the show. Brenda Walsh, Kelly's best friend, came to her rescue, comforting the poor girl in her time of need.

Lucky for Mrs. Taylor, Kelly is one strong gal. Whereas another person might have been unable to face such embarrassment, Kelly was determined to rise above it and help her mother beat the addiction. She encouraged her mother to enter a rehabilitation program.

Now that Mrs. Taylor has been sober for awhile, mother and daughter are trying to resume the close relationship they've always enjoyed. They hang out together at their pool, shop for drop-dead clothes on Rodeo Drive, and catch some rays at the Beverly Hills Beach Club.

On the romance scene, Kelly has had her share of boyfriends . . . and her share of heartbreaks! West Beverly lady-killer Steve Sanders harbors a soft spot in his heart for this headstrong but gorgeous gal, and he tries to woo her from time to time. He has his work cut out for him because Kelly thinks he is obnoxious.

And then there is Kyle, a member of the high-school football team and Beach Club volleyball coach. Kelly spotted this cute guy at the Beach Club, but after one date, he told her that he only wanted to be friends. Since then, the two have become close pals.

Kelly's best friends are Brenda Walsh and Donna Taylor. Though sometimes the pampered Kelly can't understand why her friends would rather participate in such activities as summer acting classes than join her at the Beach Club, the three are all part of what Kelly calls the "Brat Pack"—the most popular clique at school!

DAVID "DJ" SILVER

Top: Frantic freshman David "DJ" Silver is West Beverly's premiere class clown. Though his way of winning friends is to keep them laughing with his amusing antics, his heart's desire is to be a part of West Beverly's most exclusive "in" crowd. **Right:** Most days, David's wardrobe is wild enough to make the most cynical West Beverly student sit up and take notice.

There's always one in the bunch. At West Beverly Hills High School, that one is David "DJ" Silver.

A rather annoying, pesty young freshman, David is always eager to please and overly eager to fit in. He admires the "in" clique and silently wishes he could be more like them—cool. Unfortunately, his unsuccessful attempts to become a part of that crowd has made him the target of many jokes, usually because his loony antics backfire. But, David doesn't mind the laughter—he was born to be the class clown!

David suffers from a major crush on Brenda Walsh, who has fallen hard for Dylan McKay. Of course, David couldn't help but get his hopes up on the day he learned that Brenda and Dylan had parted. Imagine his disappointment upon hearing the news that the fated couple had mended their fences and gotten back together.

Though not the sort of relationship he yearns for, David has managed to stay

friends with Brenda, as he has with the other kids from the "in" crowd. David is probably closest to Donna Martin, though she would be the last to admit it. DJ and Donna became friends during an assignment in their summer acting class. The two were assigned to perform the famous balcony scene from *Romeo and Juliet* in front of the entire class. As the performance day drew near, the pair grew increasingly nervous. They just couldn't seem to get a handle on the scene. But, as usual, David had a plan.

Donna was actually worried about flunking the course, because during rehearsals, the unlikely team got little accomplished. All they did was bicker. Both realized that performing the scene straight would be a complete bomb. Then David's overactive imagination came to the rescue. He suggested that they switch parts to do this famous scene!

When the time came to show their stuff, out popped David as Juliet, complete with makeup and wig, while Donna strutted about as Romeo. The audience howled when they saw the school cut-up dressed in a gown from head to toe! Hamming it up for the class, David and Donna were an incredible success! Their teacher was amused, too, and David and Donna were off the hook—well, for a while anyway!

David annoys most of the older kids, but he is pretty harmless. Perhaps when he matures from freshman to sophomore, he'll stop trying so hard!

23

ANDREA ZUCKERMAN

Andrea Zuckerman has had a crush on Brandon Walsh since the first day she saw him. Though an unlikely couple for romance, the two are good friends and have shared a few intimate moments. Brandon is mature enough to recognize that Andrea may not be the most beautiful girl at West Beverly, but she is smart, sincere, and ambitious.

Isn't it great to be both pretty and smart!

Actually, it is only just recently that Andrea Zuckerman, editor of the student newspaper, has felt attractive. Never confident in her looks, she used to hide behind her glasses and books, preferring to be alone. But this energetic young lady has finally come into her own at West Beverly Hills High and has let her hair down to reveal her true, outspoken self. And, more than one WBHHS hunk has taken notice of the new Andrea.

Andrea has had a major crush on Brandon Walsh ever since he moved to Beverly Hills. Last spring, her secret wish came true when she and Brandon shared a passionate kiss. An unlikely couple? Maybe, but for Andrea, the kiss felt natural and right. Brandon and the Brain had become close during the school year, almost best friends. They had worked on the school paper and hung out together. Andrea even confided an important secret to Brandon about her background. It seems she had used her grandmother's Beverly Hills address to get into the prestigious high school. Her family really lived outside Beverly Hills in a middle-class neighborhood.

On the night of the spring dance, Brandon and Andrea's platonic relationship changed. It became a magic night for the two teens when they shared a deep, meaningful kiss. The next day, anxious to know how Brandon felt about her, Andrea was more than a little nervous about seeing him in school. Unfortunately, the scene didn't go as she had hoped. Obviously avoiding their true feelings, the two brushed aside their romantic encounter, calling it "just one of those things."

On the rebound from Brandon, Andrea fell into the hands of West Beverly's womanizer, Steve Sanders. Steve had agreed to help Andrea cram for the upcoming SATs, which she was determined to ace. When she found herself alone with Steve in his bedroom, events suddenly took an unstudious turn. Andrea was shocked when Steve began kissing her. Realizing it was a wrong move, she bolted from his house as fast as possible.

Top: Kelly Taylor and Andrea Zuckerman—the class beauty and the class brain. **Bottom:** Steve Sanders has tried to get close to both Kelly and Andrea, but with little success.

These days, Andrea still has a crush on Brandon but chooses to keep her feelings to herself. She silently suffers as she watches him interact with other girls. But she knows that if she and Brandon are meant to be together, then it will happen!

In the meantime, the Brain has blossomed into a beauty, and her social life has taken on a whole new dimension. Andrea has recently become close friends with Brandon's sister, Brenda Walsh, and she finally feels like she is part of the "in" crowd. Despite the importance of her new status to her self-esteem, Andrea still manages to balance her time between studying and socializing with her new friends.

DONNA MARTIN

Top: Donna Martin, like her friend Kelly Taylor, helps set the trends for the girls at West Beverly Hills High School. **Right:** However, Donna has trouble keeping pace with classmates Kelly, Brandon Walsh, and Steve Sanders when it comes to good grades and high test scores because she has a learning disability. **Opposite:** Most recently, Kelly (left) and Donna (right) have allowed Brenda (center) to become part of their clique, the "Brat Pack."

There's nothing overly special about Donna Martin. Yes, she seems to be the typical Beverly Hills teenager who owns a fancy car and a closet full of designer clothes. She spends her summer days at the Beverly Hills Beach Club and her nights cruising. And yes, she enjoys only the finer things in life: eating at the best restaurants, going to the hottest parties, and dating only handsome, wealthy boys. Nothing separates this attractive teen from the "in" crowd that she most definitely belongs to at West Beverly Hills High School. Well, almost nothing.

At school, Donna lacks one thing many of her close friends certainly do possess—good grades. Though she would be reluctant to admit it, this frustrates her, especially when she knows how much effort she puts into school. Donna has a slight learning disability, and because of it, she has to work twice as hard to keep up with her intelligent friends.

The SAT exams were extremely disappointing to Donna. She watched as her friends Kelly Taylor and Brenda Walsh crammed for the tests, and she pretended to cram along with them. But deep down, she knew she had no hope of doing well. These days, Donna is trying her best to work at her disability. Maybe by next year, her academic situation will improve and things will look brighter.

In the meantime, Donna is taking the same summer acting class as her friend Brenda. Here's hoping that she will discover a hidden talent that will compensate for any disappointment caused by her learning disability.

Despite any inadequacy she may feel in comparison to her brainy friends, there's no question that Donna Martin is considered the real style-setter of West Beverly Hills High School. Thanks to her fortunate financial situation, Donna is able to buy the coolest clothes around. A true clotheshorse, she has the taste and style to predict what will be the latest fashion trend. As thin as she is, she can wear almost anything and look dynamite!

MEET THE CAST

All of Hollywood is envious of the producers of *Beverly Hills, 90210* for discovering the hottest cast on television. From hunky Jason Priestley to stylish Tori Spelling, the *90210* gang is not only attractive but talented and experienced. These highly professional young actors are no strangers to the grind behind the glamour of Hollywood—most are veterans of past TV series while some have costarred in feature films.

Now, meet the real reason behind the success of *Beverly Hills, 90210*—the dream cast of a lifetime.

JASON PRIESTLEY

Full Name: JASON PRIESTLEY

Nickname: Jay

Birthplace: Vancouver, British Columbia

Current Residence: Woodland Hills, California

Birthdate: August 28, 1969

Height: 5'9"

Weight: 140 pounds

Hair: Light Brown

Eyes: Blue-green

Quote: "Brandon is such a nice guy...far nicer than me!"

Above: Jason Priestley and Luke Perry represent
Beverly Hills, 90210 in a celebrity softball game.
Opposite: Off the screen, Jason sports a more casual
look than he does when playing clean-cut
Brandon Walsh.

From as far back as he can remember, Jason Priestley has wanted to act. Born in Vancouver, British Columbia, Jason grew up surrounded by show business professionals. His grandfather was a circus acrobat; his father constructed sets; his mother was a singer/dancer/choreographer who once performed for the Queen; and his older sister, Justine, is an actress and model. With genes like that it's no wonder he's such a natural!

At the early age of four or five, Jason pleaded with his mother to get him into show business. It wasn't long before the very adorable youngster began winning roles in Canadian commercials and TV sitcoms. At age eight, he was cast in his very first movie—a drama for Canadian television titled *Stacey*.

His acting career moved along beautifully, but in his early teens, Jason quit the business! "I quit because I wanted to be a teenager." Jason revealed to *16 Magazine.* "I didn't want to worry about how I looked—did I look right for this part or that part?" Instead, Jason became a rebellious kid, wearing the style and copping the attitude of a punk rocker. "I jumped on the tail end of the punk movement," he told *People.* "I was

Above and opposite: Jason costarred in the short-lived sitcom *Sister Kate*, with Stephanie Beachum as a nun who takes in orphans.

into chains, black jeans, and combat boots."

Jason eventually passed through his rebellious phase and returned to acting. By age 16, he was back in show biz! Still living in Vancouver, he snagged major parts in episodes of *Danger Bay*, *Airwolf*, and *MacGyver*, as well as secondary roles in such movies as *The Boy Who Could Fly*.

While still in Canada, Jason had a recurring role as a derelict on *21 Jump Street*. With the kind of exposure a hit series brings, the demand for Jason in Hollywood increased dramatically. Soon, he found himself virtually commuting to Los Angeles from Vancouver! It was then that he decided to move to Hollywood.

At age 20, Jason finally landed the role he'd been looking for—as part of the cast of a new network sitcom! Jason was a shoe-in for the role of Todd Mahaffey on the NBC series *Sister Kate*. Unfortunately, the show was history in a matter of months, and Jason was out of a job. Unemployed, he pounded the pavement looking for his next role.

Because of Jason's short stint on *Sister Kate*, a blonde actress named Tori Spelling had developed a major crush on him! For Jason, this crush became a blessing in disguise when Tori's famous father, producer Aaron Spelling, was casting a new series titled *Class of Beverly Hills*. Tori told her father about a dynamite young actor named Jason Priestley, and the rest is history!

Today, Jason is grateful to be part of the hottest show on television. When he's not on the set, this handsome heart-throb spends the majority of his free time participating in athletics. Hockey, motorcycling, rugby, tennis, and snow skiing are among his favorites, but Jason also has a wild side to him. In fact, this smashing daredevil loves to go bungy-jumping!

SHANNEN DOHERTY

Full Name: SHANNEN MARIA DOHERTY

**Nicknames: Jason calls her Shannendoah;
Luke calls her Shando.**

Birthplace: Memphis, Tennessee

Current Residence: Los Angeles, California

Birthdate: April 12, 1971

Height: 5′ 3″

Weight: 100 pounds

Hair: Dark Brown

Eyes: Blue

**Quote: "I don't believe in hiding anything . . . why be
nice to someone's face, and then turn around
and talk all this dirt about them? . . . If you
have something to say about someone—say it
to them."**

Above: Shannen poses with her parents and her
brother. Shannen (in pigtails) played Jenny Wilder
in Michael Landon's *Little House: A New Beginning.*

At twenty, pretty Shannen Doherty
has been acting professionally for ten
years. A native of Memphis, Tennessee,
Shannen and her family moved to Los
Angeles when she was a young child. In
L.A., Shannen discovered acting.

As the story goes, she was eight-and-
a-half years old when she went to watch
her best friend audition for a children's
theater production of *Snow White and the
Seven Dwarfs.* The director of the play
asked the bright-eyed, dark-haired girl if
she would like to audition, too. Shannen
agreed and landed one of the lead roles!

She discovered that acting was exhila-
rating, and when *Snow White* ended, she
wanted more. She begged her parents to
sign her with an agent, but her parents

Shannen is fond of stylish hats.

Shannen played Kris Witherspoon on *Our House*.

were apprehensive about letting her act. They were worried that show business might corrupt her. After two years of constant pleading, they finally agreed, and within a week of signing, Shannen landed her first job—a voice-over in the animated film *The Secret of NIMH*!

Roles in television commercials followed, as did parts in various sitcoms. After appearing in an episode of *Father Murphy*, Shannen was cast in a Michael Landon series called *Little House: A New Beginning*. Her stint as a regular on that show lasted a year. She then made the rounds in Hollywood, landing role after role in episodes of various TV series, including *The Voyagers*, *The Outlaws*, *Highway to Heaven*, *Airwolf*, *Magnum*

P.I., *Life Goes On*, and *21 Jump Street*. Though she loved the work, she dreamed of getting another role as a regular on a series.

Perseverance pays off! It wasn't long before she won a terrific role on the family drama *Our House* as Kris Witherspoon. Unfortunately, *Our House* lasted less than two seasons. Shannen took the opportunity to concentrate more on her school work. At that time, she was in a private high school called Lycee Francais, trying to keep up her impressive 4.0 average.

Attending high school became a social affair for Shannen. While she says she wasn't part of one particular clique, she does confess that she had friends in all

the school cliques. "I was my own person," she told *Loud Mouth*. "I've always been a very secure person . . . My opinion is this: If you like who I am, that's great, but I'm not going to change because of you."

During high school, Shannen also took time out to do a movie she thought seemed pretty interesting after reading the script. Called *Heathers*, this black comedy was a big, big hit! Shannen played one of the three characters named Heather. Winona Ryder and Christian Slater starred in the film as the Heathers' archenemies. Shannen muses that her character Heather Duke was more like a West Beverly Hills High student than any other character she's ever played!

Right now, Shannen is lighting up TV screens as Brenda Walsh on *Beverly Hills, 90210*. It's a role she is both pleased and proud to be doing. Off the set, Shannen loves hanging out with friends such as castmate Tori Spelling. "It's fun when I get a group of friends together," she told *Teen Beat*. "Like a 'girls' day out.' Just walking around, talking about everything. That's fun."

Left and opposite: Shannen tries to play positive role models in her TV work, which is why she likes clean-cut Brenda Walsh.

LUKE PERRY

Full Name: LUKE PERRY

Birthplace: Mansfield, Ohio

Current Residence: Hollywood, California

Birthdate: October 11, 1966

Height: 5' 10"

Weight: 140 pounds

Hair: Dark Brown

Eyes: Brown

Quote: "Nonconformity is one thing that if you have to talk about it, then you're kind of conforming."

Luke Perry believes that he is generally more fun than his character, Dylan, as indicated by Luke's choice in pets—a pig named Jerry Lee.

"I could tell you how old I am," Luke Perry once told a *Rolling Stone* reporter, "but then I'd have to kill you."

Though Luke was joking, there is a serious reason for the secrecy. The producers of *Beverly Hills, 90210*, in the interest of keeping their characters young in the eyes of their fans, have asked the cast not to reveal their true ages. Though it is difficult to uncover the birthdays of some *90210* stars, Luke's fans know he was born on October 11, 1966!

Luke is from Mansfield, Ohio—a far cry from the chic life in Beverly Hills. "I don't know if I'd fit in at Beverly Hills High," Luke said in the *Beacon Journal*. "But I know that I wouldn't want to try. It takes too much of an effort to fit in. Everything is about being part of the 'in' crowd. You can't be yourself.

"I think growing up in the Midwest," he continues, "gives you a strong sense of yourself. I'm proud to be an all-American, meat-and-potatoes guy from Ohio, and being around Beverly Hills kids has only made me more proud of that. I guess I'm just not a Beverly Hills type of guy." That's for sure. Like Dylan, Luke is a true nonconformist.

Luke participates in a softball game sponsored in part by Reebok athletic shoes. Wonder if Luke got to keep the shoes he used to play in?

But that's where any similarities between actor and character end. "We share the same body," Luke told *Scene* magazine. "Unfortunately, we don't share the same clothes or car!"

After graduating from high school, Luke bummed around Ohio for a while before realizing that there was nothing there for him in terms of a future. He set off for Hollywood in search of fame and fortune. In his first three years in L.A., Luke went to plenty of auditions, but could not find any work as an actor. Instead, he made money doing odd

These shots show Luke more in character as troubled Dylan McKay. Luke likes the part he plays because Dylan is allowed to be intelligent instead of being just another pretty face.

jobs—everything from flipping burgers to spreading asphalt. Unable to open any Hollywood doors, he packed up and moved to New York City.

Smart move. New York was the place to be, for within weeks Luke landed his first professional acting job—as Ned Bates on the ABC soap opera *Loving*!

Above and opposite: While working in New York, Luke appeared in several commercials, including one for Levis 501 blue jeans. The Levis ad is one of his favorites because it is so hip and stylish. Also, he prefers to wear a more casual look, including jeans.

When his character was written off the show, Luke quickly nabbed the role of Kenny on *Another World*.

Luke lived in the Big Apple for three years, working on *Another World*, doing commercials, acting in low-budget movies (*Terminal Bliss* and *Scorchers*), and enjoying all of the cultural activities New York has to offer. He didn't even think of leaving . . . that is, until he heard about a new TV show that Aaron Spelling was creating called *Class of Beverly Hills*.

As soon as Luke read the script, he knew he wanted to play Dylan McKay. "The minute I read the part," he told the Cleveland *Plain Dealer*, "I said, 'Hey, this is really something. This is an interesting character.' I felt very strongly I could connect . . . ." And connect he has, especially with fans of the show. When the handsome *90210* star was making an appearance at a Washington hotel, he was mobbed by thousands! He had to be smuggled out in a laundry hamper to avoid being torn apart!

IAN ZIERING

Full Name: IAN ANDREW ZIERING

Nickname: The cast calls him Z-man

Birthplace: West Orange, New Jersey

Current Residence: San Fernando Valley, California

Birthdate: March 30

Height: 6′

Weight: 175 pounds

Hair: Blond

Eyes: Blue

Quote: "There's a certain dichotomy in my character [Steve Sanders]. He's on the edge of what is real and what is an illusion, which is somewhat typical of Beverly Hills."

Above: Ian often plays in celebrity tennis tournaments. **Opposite:** Here Khrystyne Haje of *Head of the Class* joins Ian on the court to wish him well.

At age 12, Ian (pronounced eye-an) signed up with a noted children's modeling and acting agency in New York City. Since the age of four, he had been trying to break into show business, but without a professional representing him, it hadn't gone well. Immediately upon signing with an agent, Ian got work modeling children's clothes for a department store in New York City. From there, he worked in a steady stream of commercials for TV and radio. For a year he was the voice of the boy on the Lucky Charms cereal commercial!

High-school life was pretty normal for Ian—nothing like the life of Steve Sanders. "My high school was nothing like West Beverly Hills High," he told *Teen Beat.* "We had kids who came from affluent families, but we also had kids from less fortunate families. In Beverly Hills, it's only middle-class to 'way up there.' At my high school, there was a popular clique, but I didn't care much to be a part of it."

Instead of trying to a part of the "in" crowd, Ian opted to be part of the swim team—a more challenging and rewarding goal. He eventually made both the swim and diving teams. When high school was

over, Ian went straight into college, enrolling at William Patterson College in New Jersey. "That was a given in my family," he told *16 Magazine*. "You go to junior high school, high school, and then college. And then you're on your own."

During college, Ian worked at his first professional acting job when he landed a role on the daytime drama *The Guiding Light*. He played Cameron Stewart for three years on the soap, until he was written off the show. A year later, Ian landed a part on another soap, *The Doctors*. Interestingly, he auditioned

against another struggling young actor—a handsome fellow by the name of Luke Perry! The two have been tight friends ever since that audition.

In addition to having regular roles on these two soaps, Ian had also appeared in the long-running soap *Love of Life*, as well as in an *Afterschool Special* entitled *Flour Babies*. This adorable, blond actor made his feature film debut in *Endless Love*, the infamous teen melodrama starring Brooke Shields.

When the opportunity to try out for the part of Steve Sanders came along, Ian headed west, auditioned, and won the much coveted role! Thrilled to be part of this special show, Ian says Steve is the role of his life. Not because he's anything like the spoiled, egotistical, rich Beverly Hills kid he plays, but because he gets to act on a "smart show" with "some of the best young talent in the business."

These days, Ian spends his free time doing everything from diving to horseback riding to playing in celebrity tennis tournaments. Since moving from New Jersey to L.A., Ian has wanted to add surfing to his list of extracurricular activities. Radical! OK, so maybe he is just a teensy bit like Steve!

Left: On the steps of his trailer, Ian studies the script between takes. **Opposite:** Aside from tennis, Ian also skis, plays soccer and baseball, and rides motorcycles and horses. His latest interest is surfing.

JENNIE GARTH

Full Name: JENNIFER EVE GARTH

Birthplace: Champaign, Illinois

Current Residence: San Fernando Valley, California

Birthdate: 1972

Height: 5'5"

Weight: 110 pounds

Hair: Blonde

Eyes: Blue

Quote: "If you work very hard and long at something, you can make it happen. But you have to have faith."

Blonde hair, blue eyes, and gorgeous. That's Kelly Taylor on *Beverly Hills 90210*. And that's also Jennie Garth, the actress who plays her.

Though born in a small farming town in Illinois, Jennie and her family moved to Phoenix, Arizona, when Jennie was a child. There she entered a few beauty pageants, met a talent scout, and made her way to Hollywood! Though this sounds like a dream come true, all fairy tales feature a little bit of pain and suffering. Jennie's story is no different.

The Garths had to relocate because Mr. Garth had suffered a heart attack and needed to live in a warm climate.

Above: Jennie poses while cast member Jason Priestley snaps a photo. **Right:** Jason and Jennie then pose for someone else's camera.

After moving a few times, and changing schools again and again, the Garths finally settled in Phoenix. Due to all the moving around, Jennie had little opportunity to make friends. Looking back, Jennie realizes that if her family had not moved south, she might never have taken up dancing or acting. Because she was so lonely, Jennie began taking dance lessons, working hard to become a good dancer and choreographer.

She also entered local beauty competitions. When she took the Miss Teen Arizona title one year, one of the judges turned out to be a talent scout, who helped Jennie focus on what she really wanted to do with her life—act. The next step was moving again—this time to Hollywood.

Jennie's mom agreed to go with her to California. The two settled in an apartment with three other people, and in less than six months, Jennie landed her first job! She was cast in a Disney series titled *A Brand New Life*, starring Barbara Eden. Following the cancellation of that series, Jennie landed parts in two other Disney movies, *Just Perfect* and *Teen Angel Returns*. On the set of *Teen Angel Returns*, Jennie met her future *90210* costar, Jason Priestley!

The role of Kelly Taylor may look like it was a cinch for Jennie to snag, but actually, the actress had to audition for the part five times! All she remembers

Of all the cast members, Jennie is the least like her character. While Kelly is selfish, Jennie is involved with many social causes.

about those long days, waiting to hear her fate, was sheer agony!

In her free time, Jennie can almost always be found with her family and friends, or working for such causes as saving the environment and supporting animal rights. In short, it's plainly obvious that Jennie is nothing like the spoiled beach bunny she plays on TV. "Kelly is simply a product of her environment," Jennie says. Maybe so, but here's a bit of juicy, hot info for you: While Brenda is certainly the main female character on the show, it is Jennie who receives the most fan mail each day!

BRIAN AUSTIN GREEN

Full Name: BRIAN AUSTIN GREEN

Birthplace: Van Nuys, California

Current Residence: Van Nuys, California

Birthdate: July 15, 1973

Height: 5'9"

Weight: 145 pounds

Hair: Brown

Eyes: Blue

Quote: "If you're not enjoying what you're doing, you shouldn't be doing it."

Multitalented Brian Austin Green was born on July 15, 1973, making him one of the youngest cast members on the show. But that hasn't stopped this dynamite guy from developing tight friendships with the other cast members.

As a child, this blue-eyed actor had always wanted to be a famous musician. (Still a budding songwriter, rapper, singer, and musician, Brian has already gained studio experience, playing music for TV shows.) Because he thought he would eventually go into the music business, his parents enrolled him in a performing arts elementary school. Out of curiosity, he also signed up for acting classes.

Above and right: Brian is a typical Southern California kid: He enjoys swimming in his pool and skateboarding around Van Nuys. **Opposite:** Brian is also a budding musician, rapper, songwriter, and singer.

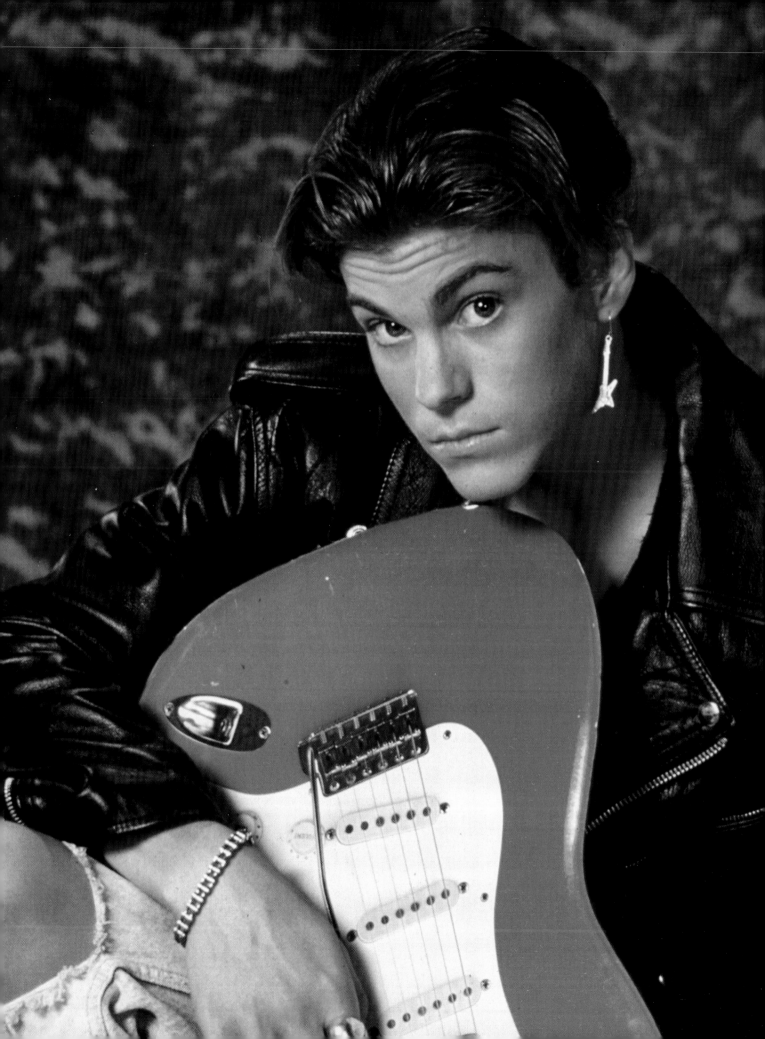

By age ten, Brian was already in demand as a young actor! Several UCLA students had recruited him to be in their student films, and after appearing in quite a few, it was obvious that Brian had been bitten by the acting bug! At that point, he got himself an agent.

Talk about being a fast worker . . . within weeks of signing with an agent, Brian was cast as Brian Cunningham on the popular prime-time soap opera *Knots Landing*! In landing the role, he beat out several more experienced actors. He has also appeared in TV commercials, done some voice-over work, and guest-starred on such TV shows as *Bay Watch*, *Highway to Heaven*, *Small Wonder*, and *The New Leave It to Beaver*.

Brian has appeared in quite a few fea-ture films as well. He was actually the star of the obscure teen flick *An American Summer*, which was not distributed nationally. He also appeared in a small part in *Kickboxer II*. His most recent film credit is a secondary role in an action drama titled *Kid*, starring C. Thomas Howell. *Kid* has just recently been released on video, and Brian's fans will not want to miss an opportunity to see him in a different kind of role.

Busier than ever, Brian works hard to annoy millions of viewers each week as pesty David "DJ" Silver on *Beverly Hills, 90210!* Brian adores working on the show and portraying his high-energy character. "My character is not your usual goody-two-shoes," he reflects. "Right from the start, I felt I could do a lot with this character."

And he most certainly has! In fact, although he isn't considered one of *90210's* hunky heartthrobs, Brian is still bombarded with fan mail. There's no question he's become a famous actor. What about his music career? Brian still hasn't given up hope that someday he'll be a famous musician, too. "And a director," he adds. "I would also like to try directing at some point."

Left and opposite: Brian played the role of Abby Ewing's son, Brian Cunningham, on the prime-time soap *Knots Landing* for several seasons.

GABRIELLE CARTERIS

Full Name: GABRIELLE ANNE CARTERIS

Birthplace: Phoenix, Arizona

Current Residence: San Fernando Valley, California

Birthdate: January 2

Height: 5'1"

Weight: 108 pounds

Hair: Light Brown

Eyes: Hazel

Quote: (When asked about her kissing scenes with Jason Priestley). "I'm pretty lucky, huh!"

Above: Gabrielle gets a boost from costar Ian Ziering. **Opposite:** Gabrielle insists the series is a ratings winner because the cast gets along so well. From left: Jason Priestley, Gabrielle, Ian, and Shannen Doherty do some publicity for the show.

Growing up, there was no question in Gabrielle's mind: She knew that she wanted to be a performer! When she was very young, she dreamed of becoming a famous ballerina. She was well on her way to fulfilling that dream when she joined the children's company of the San Francisco Ballet. Unfortunately, her dancing career never made it past a few performances. Gabrielle was considered too short to become a professional dancer.

She was not only disappointed but frustrated at being told, "You can't." Little did she know that this would not be the last time she would hear those awful words. Luckily, Gabrielle is incredibly determined and has learned to strive for her goals—regardless of what anyone tells her.

Born in Phoenix, Arizona, Gabrielle is a fraternal twin, just like Brenda and Brandon are on the show. Her twin brother's name is Jimmy. Though born in Arizona, Gabrielle considers San Francisco home. Her mother moved the family to the Golden Gate city when Gabrielle and Jimmy were still babies.

The pert young actress claims that her early years constituted "your aver-

age childhood," but in reality, Gabrielle's teen life was pretty special. An unselfish girl by nature, she spent her free time as a volunteer at a school for the deaf. She learned sign language and worked as a translator at her own school.

Her experiences at communicating in silence led to an interest in mime. At age fourteen, her miming was so good she was asked to join a professional troupe and tour Europe for the entire summer! "It was the time of my life," she confess-

es, "It was so fantastic to perform in mime. It's an international language. I loved miming in the streets!"

After high school, Gabrielle attended Sarah Larence College in New York, where she studied acting. She also spent two semesters at the Royal Academy of Dramatic Art and studied at the London Academy of Music and Dramatic Art. After graduation, Gabrielle did what every other aspiring actress does: She rented an apartment in New York City,

Above: Gabrielle claims that she is wild and crazy, unlike her character Andrea who is reserved.
Opposite: Gabrielle and Jason Priestley goof around on the set between takes. Perhaps Andrea and Brandon will get together in upcoming episodes!

got an agent, and went on millions of auditions! Luckily, Gabrielle's talents didn't go unrewarded. She won a few roles in off-Broadway plays and appeared in three *ABC Afterschool Specials—What If I'm Gay?*, *Seasonal Differences*, and *Just Between Friends*. She also played the part of a runaway teenager on the soap opera *Another World*.

Then it happened. She heard those words again: "You can't." This time, they were spoken by her own agent, who told her, "You're not pretty enough, don't expect to work much."

Devastated at first, Gabrielle finally came to the decision that she couldn't trust what this agent had told her. Mustering up every ounce of determination, she forged full speed ahead to look for an acting job despite the odds.

She headed to California during "TV pilot season" and landed an audition for a series tentatively called *Class of Beverly Hills*. Gabrielle tried out for the role of Brenda, thinking, "Wow, I could play a twin . . . I am a twin!" She was disappointed when she learned she didn't get the part, but things turned around for her when she was offered the role of brainy Andrea Zuckerman. "I totally love this character," she gushes. "And I love that she is smart and beautiful."

TORI SPELLING

Full Name: **VICTORIA DAVEY SPELLING**

Birthplace: **Los Angeles, California**

Current Residence: **Bel Air, California**

Birthdate: **May 16, 1973**

Height: **5'5"**

Weight: **100 pounds**

Hair: **Blonde**

Eyes: **Brown**

Quote: **"Sometimes, I was embarrassed because my family was rich."**

Above: Tori, as a toddler, poses with her parents, Aaron and Candy Spelling. **Opposite:** Tori at age 18: On the verge of a career in acting.

Yes, her father is the producer of *Beverly Hills, 90210.* But no, Tori doesn't receive any special attention because of it! Eighteen-year-old Tori, who plays style-conscious Donna Martin on the show, has been acting since age six. After years of guest-starring on such TV shows as *T.J. Hooker, Monsters, Saved By the Bell,* and *The Love Boat,* Tori made her feature film debut in *Troop Beverly Hills.* She likes to joke that her role in that movie was the perfect prelude to her role on *90210!*

Living in an even more lavish community than Beverly Hills—Bel Air, California—Victoria grew up in the lap of luxury. Her father, Aaron Spelling, is a very successful TV producer, responsible for such hits as *Charlie's Angels, The Love Boat,* and *Dynasty.* She rode a limo to school and kept company with some of the most famous faces in Hollywood.

Given her background, it was no surprise that Tori took to acting. Of course, it isn't hard to land parts on TV when your father is the producer, but Tori wanted to take acting lessons nonetheless. Studying at an exclusive, private school in the San Fernando Valley, Tori worked hard at her classes, juggling her

These photos chronicle Tori Spelling as she grows from childhood to teenager.

Tori has always been close to her famous father, Aaron Spelling, who is one of the most successful TV producers in Hollywood.

time between acting and schoolwork.

Tori's high-school life was probably the closest to the life of a student at West Beverly High than that of any other *90210* cast member. While she admits she was part of the hottest clique in high school, she adds that it was purely coincidental that her friends were popular. Still, Tori had a tough time in high school—especially when it came to making friends. She never knew who wanted to be her friend because of who she was

and who wanted to be her friend because of who her father was. The whole scene proved to be stressful for this blonde beauty.

When her father developed *Beverly Hills, 90210*, Tori helped him with the casting! Since she's young, hangs out with Hollywood's younger generation, and has an eye for spotting young talent, it was only natural that he asked for her help. In fact, it was Tori who recommended Jason Priestley for the role of

As an adolescent, Tori began to exhibit the fashion sense that would mark her character, Donna Martin.

Aaron Spelling not only asked his daughter's advice when casting *Beverly Hills, 90210*, he also took it!

Brandon! Tori had had a crush on the sexy actor ever since she had seen him on *Sister Kate*.

Tori also admired Shannen Doherty's work in the movie *Heathers*, and she told her dad she thought Shannen would make a perfect Brenda. She was two-for-two when her dad cast both recommendations! Tori herself had her eye on the role of Kelly Taylor, but nepotism didn't play any part in that casting. Spelling had already auditioned and cast actress

Jennie Garth in that much-coveted role. Instead, Tori landed the part of Kelly's best friend, Donna Martin. At first, Donna was just a recurring part, not a regular role, but over the course of the season, Donna developed into a full-fledged character. Now Tori is thrilled.

Off the set, Tori enjoys playing tennis and volleyball, and going to the movies—all activities she can do in her family's very own home, that beautiful mansion in Bel Air!

CRUISIN' BEVERLY HILLS

Welcome to the glamour capital of the world.
Let's cruise the elite streets, check out the elegant eateries, and browse through
the beautiful boutiques of L.A.'s most exclusive community. Let's get to know
the playground as well as the background of the gang on *Beverly Hills, 90210*.

Above: The posh community of Beverly Hills lies halfway between downtown Los Angeles and the Pacific Ocean. A leader in the worlds of fashion, finance, and entertainment, Beverly Hills tries to maintain a separate identity from other L.A. neighborhoods as indicated by this famous sign, which greets visitors on the way into town. **Top left and bottom left:** Though Beverly Hills has no beach itself, residents flock to Santa Monica, as well as other beaches, for surf and sun.

Rodeo Drive is home to some of the world's most exclusive designer shops. Dianne Anthony Kennedy, costume designer for *Beverly Hills, 90210*, often shops here for the characters' trendy clothes.

Above: Beverly Hills at Christmas takes on an even more dazzling appearance, luring shoppers with glittery lights and sparkling decorations. **Right:** The Regent Beverly Wilshire Hotel, which opened in 1928, is famous for its Italian Renaissance and Beaux Arts architecture. Located at the intersection of Wilshire Boulevard and Rodeo Drive, the hotel is a breezy walk to the city's most elegant shops, restaurants, and boutiques.

Cast member Tori Spelling lives with her parents, Aaron and Candy Spelling, in the largest, most expensive mansion built in the Los Angeles area in recent years. Located in Bel Air, the Spelling mansion reflects the ostentatious taste associated with the Beverly Hills community.

Below: Uniquely designed mansions decorate the Beverly Hills skyline. Luke Perry's character, Dylan McKay, makes his home in a neighborhood not unlike this one.

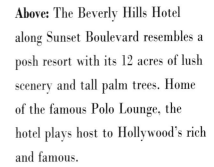

Above: The Beverly Hills Hotel along Sunset Boulevard resembles a posh resort with its 12 acres of lush scenery and tall palm trees. Home of the famous Polo Lounge, the hotel plays host to Hollywood's rich and famous.

WRITE TO YOUR FAVORITE STARS

Gabrielle Carteris
c/o Fox/Albert
8489 W. 3rd St.
Los Angeles, CA 90046

Shannen Doherty
c/o Fox TV
P.O. Box 900
Beverly Hills, CA 90213

Brian Austin Green
c/o Kelman/Arletta
7813 Sunset Blvd.
Los Angeles, CA 90046

Ian Ziering
c/o Special Artists Agency
335 N. Maple Dr.
Suite 360
Beverly Hills, CA 90210

Jennie Garth
c/o James Levy Management
3500 W. Olive
Suite 901
Burbank, CA 91505

"Beverly Hills, 90210"
c/o Fox TV
P.O. Box 900
Beverly Hills, CA 90213

Luke Perry
c/o CNA
1801 Avenue of the Stars
Suite 1250
Los Angeles, CA 90067

Tori Spelling
c/o Rogers & Cowan
10000 Santa Monica Blvd.
Los Angeles, CA 90067

Jason Priestley
c/o Freeman and Sutton
8961 Sunset Blvd.
Suite 2A
Los Angeles, CA 90069